THE DAY I DECIDED TO WRITE

Unseen, Unheard, Yet Felt

Sindhupriya Ravichandran

Made with ❤ on the BookLeaf Publishing Platform
www.bookleafpub.in
www.bookleafpub.com

Dedication

To my dad, my hero, my friend, my forever inspiration and the greatest influence in my life.
To my mom my guiding light, my shelter in the storm.
To the love of my life, my partner in every sense, my forever home.
To my loving family and friends, who taught me to love and laugh.
In memory of those who inspired me, and whose legacy lives on through these poems.

To anyone who has ever felt the power of love, laughter, and tears. May these words inspire you to find strength, hope, and joy in the journey of life.
For the quiet moments, the stillness, and the peace that we all seek.
For the love of words, and the power of poetry
To the readers, who will find a piece of themselves within these pages.

Preface

This book is a collection of moments, snapshots of my life, and the lives of those around me. Each poem is a testament to the beauty and fragility of human experience. I share my struggles, triumphs, doubts, and fears with you, in the hopes that you'll find solace in knowing you're not alone. May these poems remind you to cherish every moment, no matter how big or small.

Acknowledgements

As I reflect on the journey that has led to the creation of this poetry collection, I am reminded of the countless individuals and influences that have shaped my writing. From the teachers who have guided me, to the poets who have inspired me, and to the loved ones who have supported me, I acknowledge the complex interplay of influences and inspirations that have made this book possible.

I also acknowledge the personal struggles and triumphs that have informed my work. Thank you to my own inner wisdom for guiding me towards my truth and my voice.

I am deeply grateful to the team at BookLeaf Publishing House for their tireless efforts in bringing this collection to fruition.

And finally, to the reader – thank you for embracing these poems and making them a part of your life. May they resonate with you, inspire you, and invite you to explore the world of poetry further.

1. Echoes of Memories: My Unsung Hero

In whispers of yesterday, I hear your gentle tone,
A soothing breeze that rustles my heart, making me whole.
Memories of laughter, tears, and moments we shared,
Echoes of joy, forever etched, beyond words, beyond prayer.

Your guiding hands, a shelter from life's raging sea,
A safe haven where I could be myself, wild and free.
My dreams, my fears, my hopes, my desires, you'd hear,
And with your wisdom, calm my every fear.

Summer nights, we'd gaze up at the starry sky,
You'd point out constellations, as I'd wonder why.
The world was full of magic, mystery, and might,
With you by my side, everything felt just right.

Now, in the silence, I hear your echo clear,
A reminder of the memories we hold dear.
Though time and space may separate us now,
In my heart, our love will forever glow somehow.

In forgotten photographs, I see your smiling face,

A fleeting glimpse of joy, frozen in time's warm, golden
space.
Memories of giggles, whispers, and warm summer air,
Of all the moments we shared, beyond words, beyond
prayer.

Your hands, a map of wisdom, guiding me through life,
A gentle pressure on my shoulder, a reassuring, loving
strife.
In your eyes, a deep well of love, a reflection of my own,
A bond between us, unspoken, yet forever sewn.

Now, in the silence, I hear your voice so clear,
A whispered promise, a reminder, a love that casts out
fear.
Though time and space may separate us, now and then,
In my heart, our love will forever be, a love that
transcends, a love divine.

Dad, I'll hold on to these echoes, these memories we've
made,
A treasure trove of love, a legacy that will never fade.
In the depths of my soul, our bond will forever shine,
A love that echoes through eternity, a love that's truly
divine.

2. Through His Eyes: Seen and Loved

In the realm of love, where hearts entwine-

When your smile awakens the day,
Skies soften, and love's gentle way,
Water's symphony flows with shale's sweet tone,
Trees sway, hale and hearty, in love's sweet zone,
Birds take flight, a whirlwind's wondrous tale,
Waves swell, majestic, like a whale's dark sail,
Fishermen pause, their sale forgotten in delight,
My mistress breathes, and laughter's warm light,
Smiles escalate, joy's contagious, free and bright,
The day your smile shines, is a gift to my sight.

From the void of nowhere to the beauty of now here,
Our days transform, a vibrant mosaic, love's presence
clear,
Delusions fade, illusions lost, reality's radiant beam,
In your voice, I hear the truth, my heart's deepest dream.

3. The Daily Grind with a Twist

With umpteen hopes and chunks of balm,
Chirping sounds wake me up calm,
While the world strives for peace,
Professional life begins beyond a crease.

The wind blows me in a hustle,
Sooner I get notified by a "Ghazal",
While the replies are just above the score,
The transactions remain worth the crore.

Leisure remains unprecedented in a bean bag,
My workplace remains a temple town, beyond what I
mean,
There is little or no space for toxicity,
I buckle up my workspace with audacity.

I seldom approach a brewery,
This elevates my upbringing in a span of bravery,
There are countless days with unlimited learning,
I'm still a spendthrift with a handful earning.

There is a silver lining that keeps my winning without
whining.

And as I journey through life's ebb and flow,

I'll hold on to hope, and let my spirit glow,

For in the end, it's not the scores that matter most,

But the love, the learning, and the life I've chosen to
boast.

4. Forever Entwined

Dedicated to a love that will forever be-

A nurse with a heart of gold,
Raised siblings, young and old.
She met her soulmate, a patient so dear,
Their eyes locked hearts, and love did appear.

She hesitated at first, but love did grow,
Together they built a life to show.
A career to support, a family to raise,
Through life's ups and downs, they found their ways.

Their love was pure, their bond so strong,
Through every setback, they moved along.
She worked day and night, he stood by her side,
No ego, no pride, just love to abide.

First bike, first car, first house, and more,
Their fairytale unfolded, a love to adore.
A son and daughter born, a family complete,
Their love story inspired, a heart to greet.

But life had other plans, fate did decide,
To take the hero, leave the family to hide.

Grief and pain, a wound so deep and wide,
The daughter writes, her heart full of tears inside.

Memories linger, though feeble and faint,
The daughter holds on, through joy and painful saint.
A time machine, a wish to turn back time,
To relive the fairytale, one more rhyme.

But life moves on, though memories stay,
The daughter cherishes, the love that will always sway.
A fairytale, a love so true,
A heart that beats, with memories anew.

5. Space for Sorrow

I did search the engine for "Emotional Intelligence."
Results popped in, even at the brink of "IntelliSense."
So is my space for sorrow.

I leave no time to keep my mind idle,
As sorrow will evade with its own doodle.
So is my space for sorrow.

I decided to take help using therapy.
It covered me more like a canopy.
So is my space for sorrow.

My eyes would be the happiest as they swim in salinity.
The muscles would be the poorest as they doubt their own identity.
So is my space for sorrow.

I gear up every time with a fake smile.
The sorrow manipulates itself over an extra mile.
So is my space for sorrow.

I try to self-pat with a "This too shall pass" note.
Sooner, I would be welcomed by another sorrow with a fresh quote.

So is my space for sorrow.

Yet, in this space, I find a glimmer of strength,
A resilience that guides me, even in sorrow's length.
So is my space for sorrow, where I learn to grow.
So is my space for sorrow, where love and hope still
glow.

6. Shifting Gears, Shifting Hearts: In Neutral, In Love

Why do men adore their cars so dear,
With love and care, they wipe away each tear?
Their engines roar, their hearts beat fast.
A passion pure, that forever will last.

In garages and driveways, a love affair takes hold,
Men and their machines, a bond that never grows old.
Like a sports car on the highway, their spirits take flight,
Freedom and joy, in the driver's seat, feeling just right.

With every rev and rumble, their hearts beat strong and free,
A passion pure, that echoes, "This is my destiny."
From Fords to Ferraris, their love shines bright.
Their vehicles, an extension of themselves, a reflection of their delight.

They service, maintain, and polish with pride,
Their anger flares if someone dares to collide.
But amidst life's chaos, they drive away with ease,
Leaving others to face the emotional freeze.

The home, a haven, where love resides,

Is often neglected, while cars abide.
Homemaking, cleaning, and endless chore,
Fall on patient partners, who are still waiting for their
turn to roar.

Why do they express their love so freely and bright,
For cars, while others yearn for love's warm light?
A glance, a touch, a whispered sweet delight,
Reserved for engines, not loving hearts alight.

Do all feel this envy, this pang, this sting?
Or just a few, who wonder, and question everything?
The query haunts, like an unanswered call,
Why do they love their cars, and not love all?

But still I ask him, with a grin and a wink,
"Why so much love for car, and so little for our sink?"
He laughs and says, "It's just a guy thing."
And I say, "Well, I hope she doesn't start to sing!"
He smiles and says with a loving trend,
"My car's my best friend, and you're my BOSS, until the
very end!"

7. Porphyrophile's Ode

In a world of colors, she loves purple's hue,
My best friend, partner, in all we do.
Together we engineer in biotech's sphere,
Laughter and fun, our bond does clear.

We've chased sunsets on mountain highs,
Danced on beaches under starry skies.
From Mussoorie's hills to coastal sands,
Our adventures together forever expand.

We crash random weddings with joy and cheer,
IT pros by day, party animals clear.
Birthdays are celebrated with Metro train thrills,
Laughter and memories echoing, on joyful hills.

In bus stands, we've shared secret tales,
Celebrated traffic with joy that never fails.
At long video calls, we've crashed with glee,
Unconventional, yet unapologetically we.

At 3 am, she's my go-to friend,
Together we share secrets till morning's end.
She adores Accessorize and its charm,
A love for painting, a creative alarm.

Through her stories, I've travelled far and wide,
Visited cultures, where love and laughter reside.
Her laughter's contagious; it spreads like a flame,
Funny moments forever etched in my brain.

With surprises up her sleeve, she dazzles with fun,
Laughter echoing along stairs, on exam days' run.
Her whimsical tales, a memory aid so fine and bright,
Complicated answers, made simple, with humor's
delight.

Her laughter's contagious, a balm to my soul,
On darkest days, she makes my heart whole.
With her by my side, through life's every stage,
Together we navigate and turn each page.

Her name's inspired by ancient Greek goddesses divine,
To me, she's a goddess, with a heart that's truly mine.
Her love's non-judgmental, pure, and strong,
A treasure rare, a friendship that lasts all lifelong.

From Bangalore's gardens to Chennai's shore,
Our friendship blossoms, forever more.
Through life's ups and downs, she's always by my side,
A constant companion, my partner, my friend and guide.

And as we journey on, through life's joys and fears,
Our bond remains unbroken, through all our laughter
and tears.
For in each other's hearts, our friendship will forever
stay,
A treasure to cherish, every step of the way.

8. Voices Heard, Memories Held: The Ghats

In the Western Ghats' majestic shadow, where love shone bright,
A childhood unfolded, full of wonder, and pure delight.
I've heard the stories of a family's laughter and adventures bold,
A tale of love that echoes, forever to be told.

From freezing cold weather to peaceful, serene air,
Hot snacks and bicycle rides brought memories beyond compare.
Early morning visits to the tuition center, pitch dark and cold,
Were made warmer by mom's loving care, and hot lunches to behold.

Dad, the manager, well-known and respected too,
Had a driver to take him to the end of the road, with a journey anew.
Sweaters every day, with sunshine a rare sight,
Mom's patience and love guided them through the darkest night.

The company logo, proudly displayed in their home,

Symbolized dad's hard work, and a story to be known.
Dad's resilience and straightforward ways helped him navigate,
The harsh union meetings' gaze, with a steady heart and fate.

The mother waited for parcels from her brother's loving care,
News from family and loved ones, from a distant land to share.
The little one, born during the landslide and rain,
Was a miracle of love, bringing joy and a heart that could sustain.

Two brothers played games of their own creation,
Imagination and adventure filled every single iteration.
Their mother braved the rain, with child in one hand tight,
Umbrella shielding them, through the dark of night.

She stood strong, a beacon in the storm,
A shawl wrapped round her, a symbol of love's warm form.
Her little ones clung close, feeling safe and sound,
As she guided them through, the stormy night's profound.

The younger son waited for his elder brother's return,
All the kids cuddling him, like a baby, with love that
yearned.
Just sitting in the car, watching the tower gate,
Was a simple joy that brought happiness and a peaceful
state.

Friends from the first day of school to this very day,
Treasured memories in every single way.
Photography, a hobby born from everyday photo films,
A creative escape that brought joy and lifelong thrills.

The first bike, the first car, truck horns, and garden
delight,
Cousin visits in summer, and memories that shone so
bright.
Waiting for someone to come home, with hearts full of
cheer,
Uncle's patient driving lessons, a memory that's still
crystal clear.

Quiet birthday parties with freshly baked cakes,
36 hairpin bends, and the TN43 number, that still
awakes.
Friends from different tribes, and dad, the chief guest,
Teachers' queries, and the quiet child, memories that find
their nest.

The elder, a school leader, and the younger, the cutest
kid,
A family's love flourished in the Western Ghats' gentle
bid.
In the Hills, life unfolds with a gentle, loving pace,
A childhood filled with wonder, love, laughter, and
adventure's sacred space.

Though I wasn't there to witness it all,
I've heard the stories and felt the love that stands tall.
I feel grateful to be a part of this family's tale,
A love that's strong and memories that never fade or fail.

If only I could go back in time,
I'd walk with you on winding roads, in childhood's sweet
rhyme.
I would experience the joy and the love and the laughter
too,
And be a part of the magic that only your childhood
could do.

In the Western Ghats' embracing heart,
Life unfolded with simplicity, and love's every part.
Though years have passed, nostalgia remains,
Memories whispering, a gentle reminder of love's sweet
refrains.

I'll hold these memories, old and new,
Close to my heart, where love shines through.
In the silence, I'll hear whispers of the past,
A symphony of love, that forever will last.

9. A Home of Legacy: Four Generations Strong

In the depths of time, where memories reside,
A house stood tall, where love was the guide.
Four generations strong, a legacy of the heart,
A home where laughter, tears, and dreams never depart.

With great-grandmother's love, the seeds were sown,
In a tiny space, where roots of love were grown.
A lieutenant's salary, sent with a loving hand,
A mother's savings, that shaped a family's stand.

Childhood memories, forged by women of might,
A story woven, of love that shone like a beacon in the
night.
Neighborly kindness bridged the gap with care,
A gift of land, that showed humanity's compassionate
air.

Through years of joy and tears, the family's values shone,
A grandfather's honor, that echoed through the years,
alone.
A grandmother's strength, that raised children with care,
A parent's love, a guiding light, that illuminated every
share.

With determination in her soul, she pursued a noble
quest,
Joining medical college, to make a difference and pass
the test.
Though hardships beset her path, and struggles did
abound,
She never wavered in resolve, her family's land unbound.

The land remained, a constant love that shone,
A symbol of hope, that guided her children home.
Years went by, and children grew;
The land remained, a testament to love that forever
shines through.

Time took its toll, the house showed its age,
Broken ceilings, leaks, and a decade's turning page.
The family gathered, to revive and renew,
A housewarming celebration, to see the old house new.

A duplex, three-storeyed, with balconies wide,
A landmark of love, where memories reside.
The family's love, a radiant light,
Guided them through life's joys and darkest nights.

Siblings and cousins, a bond that will never break,
Laughter, secrets, and memories that will forever make.

A house that weathered life's joys and fears,
A home where love was the only thing that brought
tears.

Generations passed, and loved ones departed,
The house remained, a sacred heart that never faltered.
A tribute to souls, who lived and laughed and cried,
A home that heard it all, still stands with a loving sigh.

The house saw it all, from laughter to tears,
From get-together celebrations on the terrace, for years.
Evening studies in the balcony, with candles aglow,
Sunday full house, with everyone cooking, in a joyful
show.

From fights to reunions, sleepovers and dance parties
too,
Cricket matches and morning routines, memories forever
true.
Waiting for the water truck, to meet the scarcity's test,
Temple visits and yearly tours, a family's love forever
best.

Weddings, farewells, and all of life's milestones, the
house witnessed with care,
A silent guardian of the family's story, a sacred, loving
space to share.

Through every storm, the house remained strong,
A beacon of love, where memories belong.

A dream that we hold, to relive memories past,
To once again gather, and love that will forever last.
Our family's story, etched on every wall,
A legacy of love, that echoes through it all.

10. My Favorite Her

Twenty years, four months, thirteen days apart,
A precious little one arrived and stole my heart.
My soul friend, my companion, through every up and
down,
A bond so strong, a love that's forever crowned.

I watched her grow, through laughter and through tears,
Through every step, through every passing year.
She lived with me, through childhood's innocent charm,
A constant presence, dispelling alarm.

Grandparents adored her, a favorite, a shining light,
A companion, a friend, reflecting love's pure sight.
As she grew older, our bond remained the same,
No age difference mattered; she'd call me by my name.

We painted, danced, and dreamed, our spirits free and
bright,
Shared secrets, laughter, and tears, an unbreakable bond,
a love so tight.
She'd write me letters, cry when I'd travel far,
Missing each other, a love that shone like a star.

Makeup, high heels, cooking, funny faces, too,

Unconditional love, a treasure, pure and true.
Birthdays were a celebration, surprises, excitement
galore,
Twinning clothes, road games, memories we adore.

Now grown up, I miss her little self, it's just not the
same,
Wish I could turn back time, keep her tiny, innocent
flame.
Her laughter makes me happy, happy times we hold,
A treasure trove of memories, never to grow old.

I'm proud of the lady she's become, awesome, kind, and
bright,
Forever grateful for the gift of her life, shining with
delight.
No matter how old she grows, what she achieves, and
what she'll do,
My love for her will remain, forever proud, forever true.

And though she's grown, and flown away,
In my heart, she'll always stay.
My synonymous, my heart, my everything, I miss her
every day,
Hope she'll come back to me, like a little baby, in a loving
way.

And that someone, who holds my heart,

Is *my niece*, my love, my shining star from the very start.

11. A Letter to My Younger Self

A quiet soul, with fears untold,
A heart of gold, with love to hold.
You walked with care, with steps so fine,
Respecting elders, with a gentle shine.

Your favorite color is yellow bright,
A ray of sunshine, in the dark of night.
Though struggles were a part of your story,
You faced them with courage, and a heart that's glory.

You were a dreamer, with a heart so bold,
A shining star, with a story to be told.
You searched for answers, in the stars up high,
And found your strength, in a heart that wouldn't die.

Working parents, with discipline self-taught,
A beauty to behold, in a heart so fraught.
But beneath the surface, insecurities would creep,
A fragile self-image, with emotions that would seep.

You wished to be heard, to be seen and known,
To love yourself more, and let your heart be shown.
Regrets of puppy love, of chances not taken,

Of being too hard, on a heart that's shaken.

But now you see, with eyes that are wise,
That worth isn't external, but in your own surprise.
You'll rise up stronger, with a heart that's free,
Through life's challenges, and its ups and downs, you'll
see.

And when you stumble, remember:

You navigated socializing's awkward pace,
And rode out frustrations with a smiling face.
You laughed at shoelaces that knotted with play,
And rose above embarrassment, at the end of the day.

Your worth is inherent, your strength is real,
Your enoughness is unconditional and forever will
reveal.
So dear young self, with a spirit so bright,
Remember to love yourself, through morning's early
light.

Don't let the world define your worth and might,
Keep shining your light and holding on tight.
Breathe, pause, and stay true to your heart's core,
And you'll find your greatest call, a brand-new start,
forever more.

12. The Silent Scream

Hey, human, listen up!
It's me, your body,
The one you've been abusing, neglecting, and ignoring
lately.

I'm tired of being treated like a trash can day,
Filled with junk food, stress, and anxiety's toxic way.
My organs are protesting, my cells are on strike tonight,
I'm running on fumes, and my energy's dwindling to
zero light.

Remember when you were born, and I was brand new?
I took care of you and saw you through.
I nourished you, protected you, and kept you safe and
sound,
But now, it's payback time – take care of me, and turn it
around!

Shift work, partying, and endless screen time play,
Are taking a toll on me – every single day.
My sleep schedules messed up, my digestion's gone
astray,
And don't even get me started on your snacking – it's a
cry each day.

I know you think I'm invincible, a superhero, or a
machine so fine,
But trust me, I'm breaking down – it's not just a dream,
it's a sign.
I need some kindness, some self-love, and care, it's only
fair,
Or else, I'll be forced to take drastic measures – beware!

So here's the deal, human – take it easy on me, show you
care,
Feed me whole foods, move me regularly, and set me free
to share.
Give me sleep, give me rest, and give me some fun, every
day,
Or else, I'll be the one who's done, and gone away.

*P.S. Don't make me send you a strongly-worded letter, I
pray,*
*From the Department of Internal Affairs – it won't be
pretty, okay!*

13. Beyond the Frame

With love as the anchor, simplicity as the guide,
Roles were clear, with heart and home side by side.
Home-cooked meals, a haven of peace,
Gravy, veggies, idly powder, a simple release.

But now, expectations rise,
A flavorful journey, with recipes that surprise.
Culinary expertise, a must-have skill,
From American to Italian, Chinese to Indian, and more to
fulfill.

Beyond the kitchen, a world of responsibilities awaits,
Project management at work, and family schedules to
create.
Driving, dropping, picking up, through hectic schedules
and frantic dates,
Teaching, guiding, mentoring, through each passing
day's debates.

From NEET to IIT, and competitive exams too,
Guiding kids through studies, with patience shining
through.
Care for both sides, parents dear and old,
Supporting family, with love to hold.

A professional, with advice for one and all,
Current affairs, medicine, and more to enthrall.
A thousand unseen tasks, that only they can recall,
A beauty, with a heart that stands tall.

House like a museum, spotless, shining bright,
Smile through tiredness, day and endless night.
Always on call, patient, and strong,
A tribute to the ones, who carry on.

And in the silence, they hold it all,
The *women*, with a love that beats through it all.

14. The Power of Now

In the quantum realm, where thoughts are the spark,
We manifest our reality, with every intentional embark.
At 11:11, the universe aligns with our heart's desire,
Connecting our subconscious mind, with our deepest
soul on fire.

Like a hologram, our reality's designed
By the thoughts and emotions, that we've carefully
aligned.
We're the architects of our fate's design,
With every thought, we create, and manifest our state's
prime.

The power of manifestation, is a superpower we hold
dear.
A tool to create our reality, and manifest our heart's
clear.
It's not just about getting, what we want and desire's
flame,
But also about aligning, with our higher heart's sacred
name.

In relationships, we manifest love and harmony,
By aligning our energies, and resonating with symphony.

We attract what we are, in every single way,
So let's embody love, and manifest a brighter day.

But beware of manifestation experts, who claim to hold
the key,
For true power lies within, and is available to you and
me.
Don't give away your power, to those who claim to
guide,
For you are the master of your fate, and the captain
inside.

Like a lucid dreamer, we can shape our reality's stage,
With every thought, we create, and manifest our clarity's
gauge.
We're the dreamers of our fate's narrative,
With every intention, we craft our realities predictive.

To manifest our desires, we must first align our soul,
With the vibration of our heart, and make our spirit
whole.
We must let go of fear, and trust in the divine,
And have faith that our desires, will manifest in perfect
time.

As we manifest our reality, let's transcend the norm,
With thoughts that illuminate, a brighter world to form.

Let's harness our intentions, to craft a world of splendor,
Where love, kindness, and compassion, forever flourish
and surrender.

15. Inner Strength

Within every soul, a fortress lies.
We rise, reborn, and find our inner life.
Inner strength that heals, and never dies,
From physical pain to mental strife.

We brave love's storms, and emerge unbroken and
strong.
Overcoming breakups, grief, and righting wrong,
we shatter stigmas, and smash the walls that are long.
Reaching goals, and breaking barriers, where we all
belong.

For women, who spread their wings to chase their
dreams,
famous or unknown, we're all on this quest.
And men, who toil to give their families life's themes,
to survive, to thrive, and be our absolute best.

Our resilience and courage, incomparable and bright,
guides us through life's journey, day and endless night.
You are just there, just wait for your moment to take
flight.
When it does, your journey will be worth it, in the
morning light.

Keep moving forward; your strength will carry you
through.
Your destination awaits, and your journey will be worth
the fray.
You are enough; your inner strength, a beacon shining
true.
Ride its wave, trust its power, and you'll reach your
shore, come what day.

16. Doorstep Delights

Decades passed, and the world's pace did quicken,
Longing for distant goods, now just a finger's flickin'.
From country to doorstep, life has evolved with ease,
A convenience revolution, if you please.

Our grandmothers would marvel at this modern feat:
Groceries delivered, a luxury to repeat.
Our mothers would smile, recalling days of old,
When food delivery was a dream, yet to be told.

We've lost the charm of shopping's sensory delight,
Browsing stores, and catching a wonderful sight.
But gained the ease of instant gratification's sway,
A trade-off we make, every single day.

Remember those childhood days,
of trying on shoes with joyful glee,
Strolling around the store, wild and carefree.
The authenticity of buying has changed, it's true to see,
But with every boon, comes a bane, for you and me.

So let's be kind and grateful for the delivery crew,
Working hard to bring us joy, and see us through.
May the joy of shopping's past stay close to our heart,

And appreciate the love, that travels many miles to start.

For in the boxes and bags, that arrive with gentle smiles,
We find a connection, that goes beyond the miles.

17. Devotion's Essence

Since childhood's curious eyes,
I've pondered prayers and devotion's surprise.
What is devotion? What is prayer's call?
Questions that lingered, through it all.

People follow traditions, passed down the line,
From generation to generation, a heritage divine.
They visit temples, churches, mosques, and more,
Each with their own rituals, a unique faith to adore.

But amidst the differences, a common thread is spun,
A yearning for connection, with something greater than
one.
A superpower that guides, comforts, and sets free,
A mystery that's felt, but can't be seen, you see.

Fear, devotion, respect – a discipline is born,
From fasting, penance, to worship's gentle morn.
The body's pushed to limits, through pain and through
strife,
To reach a higher state, where love and peace thrive in
life.

From cracking an interview, to healing someone's pain,

Prayers are whispered, a universal language that remain.
For a loved one's safe return, or a heart that yearns to
gain,
Prayers are a plea, a hope, a heart that beats with love's
refrain.

Kids and elders, each with wishes true and bright,
Prayers are a part of life, a ritual that shines with new
light.
In every moment, a prayer is born to share,
A cry, a whisper, a thank you, a heartfelt prayer to spare.

In a world of debate, where faiths collide and roam,
I sense a superpower, deep within the earth's gentle
home.
The five elements – earth, air, fire, water, and space,
Connect us all, a bond that's hard to replace.

And so I'll hold on to this truth I've found,
That devotion's essence is love, without a sound.

18. From Postcards to Posts

We travel far and wide to post and share with glee.
Our Instagram followers must know we're living free!
We climb the highest peaks to take a selfie grand,
And risk our lives for a like from a stranger's hand.

From roads not taken to roads we frequently roam,
Our lives are a journey with trips to explore back home.
Bus rides, train rides, with crowds all around so bright,
We're traveling like crazy, with no time to spare tonight!

Couples on romantic getaways, with love in the air so
free,
Solo travelers seeking solace in the peace that's meant to
be.
We travel to rejuvenate, to break the daily pace,
But the pressure to conform leaves us with a worried
face.

We spend more on dressing up than the trip itself, it's
true,
Just to take that perfect selfie, with a pose or two.
Couples' reels and shorts, with lovey-dovey eyes so bold,
Pinterest-perfect pictures, with hashtags that shine with
gold.

We're caught up in the hype of the digital dream so high,
To post, to share, to like, and to follow, with a fervent
sigh.
We're traveling for necessity, for relaxation too,
But nowadays it's a compulsion, with a price that's hard
to break through.

Just imagine paying for flights with a cost that's hard to
bear,
What joy, oh boy, it's a travel trap that's just not fair!

So, let's take a step back and remind ourselves with a
grin,
Travel's for the soul's peace, not just to please the kin.

And when you're on that trip, with your phone in hand
so tight,
Just remember, the best views are the ones that shine so
bright!

So put down your phone, and breathe in the air so fresh
and clean,
And don't forget to laugh, and show off your silly hair,
and make some memories unseen!

19. Sunday's Stress Blues: Monday's Eve

The Sunday Scaries, oh what a fright!
A feeling of doom, on a Sunday night.
The weekend's ending, and Monday's near,
My anxiety's screaming, "Oh no, not here!"

My inbox is bursting, emails galore,
Meetings and deadlines, I'm a nervous wreck once more.
My to-do list is never-ending, it's a chore,
I'm stressed just thinking about it, and I'm not sure
what's in store.

Sundays are for relaxing, or so I've been told,
But my mind is racing, my heart is cold.
I think of all the things I haven't done,
Chores and workouts, and social fun.

Fear of the unknown, it's a scary thing,
A new week's looming, with problems that sting.
Societal pressures, they get to me,
Busyness equals success, or so it seems to be.

So here's to the Sunday stress, and all the anxiety it
brings,

May our Mondays be gentle, and our weeks take wing!
But till then, I'll just sit here and fret,
And hope that my coffee is strong enough to get me
through it, yet!

I've had these scaries since school days old,
When will a Sunday be worry-free? Maybe when I'm
old!

20. The Language of Empathy

At turtle's pace, a honking horn,
A test of patience, a lesson to learn.
A sticker on the car, a message so clear:
"Physically challenged; Please be patient, dear."

In an instant, calm took its place,
A sense of peace, a smile on my face.
Empathy and kindness, a new path to pace,
A chance to slow down, and find my inner space.

I slowed down, and let the car pass by,
A small act of patience, a heartfelt sigh.
We all bear invisible scars, unseen by the eye,
And fight battles that others may never try.

Perhaps someone's struggling with a weight so bold,
And needs a gentle hand to help their heart unfold.
Let us honor the invisible struggles we face,
And treat each other with gentle kindness and space.

For everyone's fighting a battle we can't define,
And compassion and empathy can be a healing shrine.
So let's take a breath, and let love radiate,

Let's offer a listening ear, and a comforting state.

Let's be the safe haven where hearts can heal,
And let's rise above with love that makes us real.
In this final moment, let's make a conscious choice,
To see the beauty in each other's poignant voice.

Let's hear the whispers of the heart's deepest pain,
And let's respond with love that heals and remains.
As we part, may love and kindness be our way,
May we walk in light, and brighten each new day.

And may goodness follow us, come what may.

21. Wooden Reflections

In the quiet of the wooden space,
I find my thoughts, and a sense of peaceful place.
Fading stress, in wood's warm hold, I am found.

The wooden grain, a story tells,
Of moments past, and memories that dwell.
Healing soul, with wood's gentle might, I am found.

In the stillness of the wooden room,
I discover solace, and a sense of peaceful bloom.
Embracing life, with wood's warm heart, I am found.

The wooden texture, a sensation deep,
Echoes emotions, and memories I keep.
Finding peace, in wood's gentle touch, I am found.

And as I leave this wooden nest,
I carry peace with me, and let my spirit rest.
Wrapped in wood's warm, gentle love, I am forever
found.

22. Brewing Bonds

In India's offices, aromas rise:
Cardamom and coffee, a fragrant surprise.
A symbol of warmth, care, and hospitality's art,
A steaming cup of comfort, shared among colleagues'
heart.

Coffee lovers gather, cups in hand, with cheer;
The gurgle of the brew, a soothing sound so clear.
Cappuccinos to lattes, flavors bold and bright,
Conversations flow, friendships forge, in morning's
warm light.

Tea enthusiasts smile, with knowing glances wide,
The clinking of cups, a joyful, lively tide.
Masala chai to green tea, sipped with joyful sound,
Tensions flee, like morning dew, on solid ground.

Office kitchen or café, cozy spaces abound;
The hum of the espresso, a friendly, welcoming sound.
Deadlines, meetings, emails, stress's heavy load,
A steaming cup of comfort, helps colleagues reconnect,
on solid road.

Tea and coffee culture, a treasured find, so true,

A thread of connection, weaving colleagues anew.
Hospitality, respect, appreciation, in every shared sip,
Colleagues, old and new, friendship grows, with love's
gentle grip.

Diversity's vibrant fabric, cultures blend, shine bright;
Tea and coffee culture, a common language, spoken with
delight.
Unity, a rich brew, love, care, kindness overflowing free,
A steaming cup of comfort, shared space, warm
harmony.

And if you're still awake, after all this tea and coffee
cheer,
Congratulations! You're an office superstar, and your
caffeine levels are clear!

23. Illuminating My Path

I offer you these words, in hopes they find a home within–
Incredible in every way, I shine so bright.
Inspiring myself with my heart, and my inner light.
Intelligent and insightful, with a mind so bold.
Innovative and imaginative, with a spirit to unfold.

Infectious is my laughter, and my smile so wide.
Influencing my own path, with my kindness inside.
Invaluable are my contributions, to my own life's design.
Inspiring a brighter future, with a heart that's truly mine.

Inwardly, I ignite my soul, illuminating my way.
I am the architect of my dreams, every single day.
I am the master of my fate, the captain of my soul.
I am unstoppable, and my spirit makes me whole.

I am a beacon of hope, a shining star in the night,
I inspire others to rise, and shine with all their might.
I am a reminder that dreams can become my fate,
I am living proof that greatness is within, don't hesitate.

P.S. May these lines be a treasured friend, that stays with you until the very end.